CONTENTS

Introduction

INTRODUCTION

As time goes by, we either find ourselves in the middle of a housing market 'boom' or a 'bust'. Currently, at the time of writing, we are experiencing a continuing decline in property prices. However, notwithstanding market conditions, the process of buying and selling a home remains probably the single most important activity undertaken by individuals in their lifetime. The money and effort involved means that it is a process that must be carried out effectively and with a clear knowledge of the elements involved.

When buying or selling a home, particularly buying, you will liase with a whole number of people, professional or otherwise: solicitors, estate agents, finance brokers, surveyors, banks and building societies and so on. All of these people play a vital role in the house purchase/sale transaction. All of these parties involved will have many years experience of property and not all of them will be acting in your own best interests.

Very often, the person who owns the property or who wishes to purchase a property is the one with the least knowledge of the process and is the one who stands to lose the most. When initially looking for a property, wrong decisions are made. The price paid for a property is quite often too high, with disastrous consequences later on. The condition of the property may leave a lot to be desired. There are many stories of people losing out on this single most important transaction. Unfortunately, it is a fact that if mistakes are made at the outset then you might spend the rest of your life recovering from the consequences.

This book also covers buying a property abroad and is meant to be of help to those who have decided to invest in a property overseas for one reason or another. Like all areas of life, knowledge is a precious asset and can help you make informed decisions. This book will go some way to assist you in being able to make informed decisions and to understand more about the process of buying and selling a property.

****

1

Buying a Home-Looking for a Home

Obviously, where you choose to buy your house will be your own decision. However, it may be your first time and you may be at a loss as to where to buy, i.e. rural areas or urban areas, the type and cost of property or whether a house or flat. There are several considerations here:

Area

Buying in a built up area has its advantages and disadvantages. There are normally more close communities, because of the sheer density. However, it is true to say that some built up areas have become fragmented by population movement, "Yuppification" etc. Local services are closer to hand and there is a greater variety of housing for sale. Transport links are also usually quite good and there are normally plenty of shops.

Disadvantages are less space, less privacy, more local activity, noise and pollution, less street parking, more expensive insurance and different schooling to rural environments. The incidence of crime and vandalism and levels of overall stress are higher in built up, more urban areas. This is not the case with all built up areas. It is up to the buyer to carry out research before making a commitment. If you are considering buying in a rural area, you might want to consider the following: there is more detached housing with land, more space and privacy. However, this can be undermined by the "village" syndrome where everyone knows your business, or wants to know your business. There is also cleaner air and insurance premiums can be lower. Disadvantages can be isolation, loneliness, lower level of services generally, and a limited choice of local education.

Choosing your property

You should think carefully when considering purchasing a larger property. You may encounter higher costs, which may include:

- Larger, more expensive, carpeting
- More furniture. It is highly unlikely that your existing furniture will suit a new larger home.
- Larger gardens to tend. Although this may have been one of the attractions, large gardens are time consuming, expensive and hard work.
- Bigger bills
- More decorating
- Higher overall maintenance costs

Valuing a property

In the main, buyers will leave it to estate agents to offer a fair price, or market price for the house. In a period of spiralling house price inflation which is now thankfully over, values were seemingly plucked out of the air. If you want to compare estate agents valuations with others then you can access one of the websites, such as www.hometrack or rightmove in order to gain a comparative value. Other sites are the Halifax, Nationwide, the Royal Institute of Chartered Surveyors, the National Association of Estate Agents and the Land Registry. You can also gain an idea of the valuation by looking in estate agents windows and assessing similar properties.

Purchasing a flat

There are some important points to remember when purchasing a flat. These are common points that are overlooked. If you purchase a flat in a block, the costs of maintenance of the flat will be your own. However, the costs of maintaining the common parts will be down to the landlord (usually) paid for by you through a service charge. There has been an awful lot of trouble with service charges, trouble between landlord and leaseholder. It has to be said that many landlords see service charges as a way of making profit over and above other income, such as ground rent, which is usually negligible after sale of a lease.

Many landlords will own the companies that carry out the work and retain the profit made by these companies. They will charge leaseholders excessively for works which are often not needed. The 1996 Housing Act (as amended by the Commonhold and Leasehold Reform Act 2002) attempts to strengthen the hand of leaseholders against unscrupulous landlords by making it very difficult indeed for landlords to take legal action for forfeiture (repossession) of a lease without first giving the leaseholder a chance to challenge the service charges. Be very careful if you are considering buying a flat in a block – you should establish levels of service charges and look at accounts. Try to elicit information from other leaseholders. It could be that there is a leaseholders organisation, formed to manage their own service charges. This will give you direct control over contracts such as gardening, cleaning, maintenance contacts and cyclical decoration contracts. Better value for money is obtained in this way. In this case, at least you know that the levels will be fair, as no one leaseholder stands to profit.

Leasehold Reform Act 1993 as amended by the Commonhold and Leasehold Reform Act 2002

Under this Act, all leaseholders have the right to extend the length of their lease by a term of 90 years. For example, if your lease has 80 years left to run you can extend it to 170 Years. There is a procedure in the above Act for valuation. Leaseholders can collectively also purchase the freehold of the block. There is a procedure for doing this in the Act although it is often time consuming and can be expensive. There are advantages however, particularly when leaseholders are not satisfied with management.

Viewing properties

Before you start house hunting, draw up a list of characteristics you will need from your new home, such as the number of bedrooms, size of kitchen, garage, study and garden. Take the estate agents details with you when viewing. Also, take a tape measure with you. Assess the location of the property. Look at all the aspects and the surroundings. Give some thought as to the impact this will have in your future life. Assess the building. Check the facing aspect of the property, i.e., north, south etc. Check the exterior carefully. Earlier, I talked about the need to be very careful when assessing a property. When you have made your mind up, a survey is essential.

Look for a damp proof course - normally about 15cm from the ground. Look for damp inside and out. Items like leaking rainwater pipes should be noted, as they can be a cause of damp. Look carefully at the windows. Are they rotten? Do they need replacing and so on. Look for any cracks. These should most certainly be investigated. A crack can be symptomatic of something worse or it can merely be surface. If you are not in a position to make this judgement then others should make it for you.

Heating is important. If the house or flat has central heating you will need to know when it was last tested. Gas central heating should be tested at least once a year.

All in all you need to remember that you cannot see everything in a house, particularly on the first visit. A great deal may be being concealed from you. In addition, your own knowledge of property may be slim. A second opinion is a must.

Buying an old house

If you are considering purchasing an older house and making improvements then there are a number of things to think about: consider whether your proposed alterations will be in keeping with the age and style of the house, and neighbouring houses, particularly in a terrace. A classic mistake is that of replacing doors and windows with unsympathetic modern products. Again, salesmen will sell you anything and quite often won't provide the correct advice. If appropriate, you should consider contacting the Victorian Society or the Georgian Group for advice on preserving your home. Both offer leaflets to help you carry out appropriate restoration. It is often a good idea to employ an architect or surveyor to oversee any alterations you are considering. For local contractors contact the Royal Institute of British Architects or Royal Institute of Chartered Surveyors.

Renovation grants

These may be available from local authorities, although there are stringent requirements. They are means tested and the higher your income the more you are expected to pay. For further details you should contact your local authority direct.

Disabled facilities grant

A grant may be available to adapt a property for a disabled person, for example improving access into and around the home and adapting existing facilities within it. These grants are mandatory, but a discretionary grant is available to make a property suitable for the accommodation, welfare or employment of a disabled person. A leaflet, generally entitled Help for Disabled People with Adaptation and Other works, which can be obtained from your local authority, provides basic information.

Equalities Act 2010

The Equality Act 2010, with effect from October 2010, has

16

introduced an obligation on all landlords to ensure that, if a disabled person requests it, suitable disabled access to common parts, and within common parts is available. Again, information is available from the local authority.

Planning permission

If you are considering alterations of a significant nature, either internal or external, you may need planning permission from your local authority. You may need planning permission if you plan to change the look or external aspect of the building or if you are intending to change the use.

You are allowed to carry out some work without planning permission, so it is worth contacting the local authority. You should also ask about building regulations. These are concerned with the materials and methods of building adopted. Regulations for work carried out in conservation areas are strict. The building control department at your local authority will be able to advise you about building regulations.

Buying a listed building

Buildings of architectural or historical interest are listed by the Secretary of State for National Heritage following consultation with English Heritage, to protect them against inappropriate alteration. In Wales, buildings are listed by the Secretary of State for Wales in consultation with CADW (Heritage Wales). In Scotland, they are listed by the Secretary of State for Scotland, in consultation with

Historic Scotland. If you intend to carry out work to a listed building, you are likely to need listed building consent for any internal or external work, in addition to planning permission. The conservation officer in the local planning department can provide further information.

Buildings in conservation areas

Local authorities can designate areas of special architectural or historical significance. Conservation areas are protected to ensure that their character or interest is retained. Whole towns or villages may be conservation areas or simply one particular street. Strict regulations are laid down for conservation areas. Protection includes all buildings and all types of trees that are larger than 7cm across at 1.5m above the ground. There may be limitations for putting up signs, outbuilding or items such as satellite dishes. Any developments in the area usually have to meet strict criteria, such as the use of traditional or local materials.

This also applies to property in national parks, designated Areas of Outstanding Natural Beauty and the Norfolk or Suffolk Broads.

Whether or not a property is listed or is deemed to be in a conservation area will show up when your conveyancer carries out the local authority search.

Buying a new house

There are a number of benefits to buying a new house. You have the advantages of being the first occupants. There should not be a demand for too much maintenance or DIY jobs, as the building is new. There will however be a defects period which usually runs for 6 months for building and 12 months for electrical mechanical. During this period you should expect minor problems, such as cracking of walls, plumbing etc, which will be the responsibility of the builder.

Energy loss will be minimal. A new house today uses 50 per cent less energy than a house built 15 years ago; consider the savings over an older property. An energy rating indicates how energy efficient a house is. The National House Building Council uses a rating scheme based on the National Energy Services Scheme, in which houses are giving a rating between 0 and 10. A house rated 10 will be very energy efficient and have very low running costs for its size. Security and safety are built in to new houses, smoke alarms are standard and security locks on doors and windows are usually included.

When the housing market is slow developers usually offer incentives to buyers, such as cashback, payment of deposit etc. Sometimes they offer a part exchange scheme. These are definitely worth looking into. However, with part exchange you may not get the price you were looking for.

Building Guarantees

All new houses should be built to certain standards and qualify for one of the building industry guarantees. These building guarantees are normally essential for you to obtain a mortgage and they also make the property attractive to purchasers when you move. A typical Guarantee is the National Housebuilding Council Guarantee (NHBC).

Websites for housebuilders

Most developers have their own websites with details and picture of their developments. These include both new properties and refurbished. In addition there are several websites that specialise in new properties only. Two such sites are:

www.freeagents.co.uk

www.newhomesnetwork.co.uk

Buying a Rented House-Right to Buy

If you rent your house from your council, you will be able to buy it at a discount under Right to Buy legislation. If you live in a new town, a housing association or housing association trust, you would need to make enquiries, as many are exempt. In order to buy:

- You must have a secure tenancy
- You must have spent at least five years as a tenant of your current landlord or another right to buy landlord
- The house or flat must be a separate dwelling and your only or principle home.

The discount will vary according to length of tenancy and type of property. For further details you should contact your landlord. A scheme, called Statutory Purchase Grant, is also available to assist those tenants of public sector landlords without the right to buy to purchase their homes. The discount is not so generous as the right to buy, usually ranging from £10,000-£13,000. Again details should be obtained from your landlord

Shared/part ownership property

There are properties available on a shared/part ownership basis, usually from housing associations. Local Authorities also provide such schemes, although rarely. The main principle is that you buy a percentage of the property, say 50% and you rent the rest, with a service charge if a flat. As time goes by you can "staircase up" to 100% ownership. This is a scheme specially designed for those who cannot meet the full cost of outright purchase in the first instance. Usually, your total monthly outgoings are smaller than they would be if you purchased outright.

Social Housing providers run a range of different schemes each year, largely depending on Government requirements. For further details you should contact a large housing association in your area who will provide you with current schemes on offer and point you in the right direction.

Self-build property

Self-build is another option for obtaining a new home. However, it is time consuming and not for the faint hearted. You need to be organised and to have organised the finances and your work programme. Usually the biggest problem is finding a suitable plot of land. There is a lot of competition. It also means that you will, unless you employ an agent, be charged with supervising a number of skilled craftsmen. Self-build usually works out cheaper than buying off a developer but it is certainly not an easy option. For more information and advice check out the following websites:

www.homebuilding.co.uk
This is run by the publishers of homebuilding and renovation magazine which is the leading magazine for homebuilders. The site is magazine style with lots of articles and also a link to www.plotfinder.net. This is a recently established database of land for sale and houses to renovate. There is an annual subscription cost, currently £35.

www.buildstore.co.uk
This site is owned by a group of venture capitalists, individuals and companies involved in the self build market. Again, there is a mix of articles and also adverts plus a site similar to plotfinder.

www.ebuild.co.uk
This site is published by specialist publisher's webguides on line. The site includes a directory of suppliers from architectural salvage to waste disposal with links to useful sites.

www.npbs.co.uk
This is the site of Norwich and Peterborough Building Society, who offer mortgages for self build projects. The loan for self-build is

released in stages linked to the building of the property. It is worth checking to see if these mortgages are on offer.

Now read the Key Points from Chapter 1 Overleaf.

****

Key Points From Chapter One

- When looking for a house, consider essential points such as area and services.

- Think carefully about costs involved and also work if you are considering buying a larger property.

- When purchasing a flat, consider maintenance charges.

- Before viewing, draw up a list of characteristics you will need from a house or flat.

- There are a number of advantages to buying a new house, such as new construction and minimal energy loss.

- Other schemes available include self-build housing

2

The Role of Estate Agents in Buying and Selling Property

Estate Agents

What to expect from an estate agent:

- Advice on the selling or asking price of a house or flat - they know the local market
- Advice on the best way to sell (or buy) and where to advertise; they should discuss an advertising budget with you
- If selling, a meeting to visit, assess and value your home and also to take down the particulars of your home. The Property Misdescriptions Act, which arose out of the bad old days of the 1980's, prevents agents from using ambiguous statements to enhance the sale of the property. You should look at the points carefully as people who are disappointed after reading such a glowing report will not purchase.
- They may ask for details of recent bills, such as council tax and electricity. They should also be willing to give advice on fixtures and fittings included in the sale.
- They should be willing to show potential buyers around your home if you are not available.

- Don't expect to have to pay for a for-sale board although some lenders will try to make a charge.

Choosing an agent if selling

Consider the following points:

- They ought to sell your type of property or specialise in one particular area of the market
- They should be a member of one of the professional bodies such as the National Association of Estate Agents, the Royal Institution of Chartered Surveyors, The Incorporated Society of Valuers and Auctioneers, The Architects and Surveyors Institute or the Association of Building Engineers.
- Obtain quotes of fees, including the basic charge and any extras you might have to pay for, such as advertising in specialist publications.

Choose at least two agents to value the house, if instructing an agent.

Sole agency selling.

Offering an agent sole agency may reduce the fee. This can be done for a limited time. After this you can instruct multiple agents. With sole agency you can sell privately, although you may still be liable for the sole agent's fee.

Joint sole agents

With this arrangement, two or more agents co-operate in the house sale and split the commission. The agents may charge a higher commission in this case.

Multiple agency

This means that you have several agents trying to sell your home, but only pay the agent who sells your property.

Buying property using the internet

There are a number of websites that also detail properties, some are independent and some are owned by the large players.

The following are a selection of the main sites:

www.rightmove.co.uk.
This is one of the largest sites, jointly owned and run by Halifax, Royal Sun Alliance, Connell and Countryside assured Group. They jointly claim to represent more than 170,000 properties covering 99% of UK postcodes. The main function of this site is as a property search site, enabling people to search for property by name of area and postcode.

Each property has a reference number and will have a photo and details. These can be obtained by clicking on the property. There is much useful information, including room sizes.

www.fish4.co.uk
This site is owned by a consortium of local newspapers groups and

came into being in 1999. They claim that there is over 174,000 properties for sale and rent and it is updated daily. Fish is, basically, online advertising, with sections covering many activities, including property.

www.zoopla.co.uk
The claims of this website are that it can help the buyer to find a property, move home and settle in.

www.primelocation.co.uk
This site was launched in 2000 by a consortium of estate agents. This site deals with more expensive properties.

Selling property using the internet

Although estate agents are still the main avenues for selling property, as we have seen, the web now plays a more significant part. In addition to the websites detailed, almost all agents now have their own website. This is really an electronic shop window where your property is displayed. Buyers interested in your property should be able to e-mail the estate agent directly for a viewing.

Now read the key points from chapter 2.

Key points from chapter 2

- Estate agents have a number of roles. However, the main function is to guide the buyer/seller through the process from beginning to end.

- Make sure that you choose the appropriate agent if selling. Make sure that the agent is a member of a professional body.

- You will need to consider whether you wish to sell through more than one estate agent.

- There are a number of websites dealing with buying and selling property. This is often a cheaper way of purchasing or selling.

3

Buying a Property-The Practicalities

Considerations when buying a house or flat

Budget

Before beginning to look for a house you need to sit down and give careful thought to the costs involved in the whole process. The starting point is to identify the different elements in the overall transaction.

Deposit

Sometimes the estate agent will ask you for a small deposit when you make the offer (see Estate Agents, chapter 2). This indicates that you are serious about the offer and is a widespread and legitimate practice, as long as the deposit is not too much, £100 is usual. The main deposit for the property, i.e., the difference between the mortgage and what has been accepted for the property, isn't paid until the exchange of contracts. Once you have exchanged contracts on a property the purchase is legally binding. Until then, you are free to withdraw. The deposit cannot be reclaimed after exchange.

Until recently, and the onset of the current recession, banks would normally lend up to 95% of the purchase price of the property.

However, particularly now, even though a few banks are willing to lend up to 95% the less you borrow the more favourable terms you can normally get from bank or building society. It has to be said that in the period leading up to the 'credit crunch' we were in a situation where banks loaned money to all and sundry at up to 125% of the value of the home plus exaggerated income multiples. Banks have now tightened up their lending criteria considerably. It is now likely that banks will insist on larger minimum deposits. This will vary with the bank or building society and you should also scan the Sunday newspapers in particular for details of best buys for mortgages.

Stamp duty

The following are stamp duty rates:

Up to £125,000	Zero
Over £125,000 to £250,000	1%
Over £250,000 to £500,000	3%
Over £500,000 to £1 million	4%
Over £1 million to £2 million	5%
Over £2 million from 22 March 2012	7%
Over £2 million (purchased by certain persons including corporate bodies) from 21 March 2012	15%

Tax for properties held offshore

HMRC has announced, at the time of writing, March 2013, that an annual levy will now be made on properties held in British and Offshore companies, costing £2million or more. This is a measure to tackle tax avoidance. Those homes valued at between £2m-£5m will have to pay £15,000 per year; those between £5m-£10m will be taxed at £35,000; those with values of between £10m-£20m will pay £70,000 per year. owners of homes above £20m per year will have to pay £140,000 per year.

Whilst this is not likely to affect readers of this book, it is always better to be aware of such changes.

Other costs

A solicitor normally carries out conveyancing of property. However, it is perfectly normal for individuals to do their own conveyancing. All the necessary paperwork can be obtained from legal stationers and it is executed on a step-by-step basis. It has to be said that solicitors are now very competitive with their charges and, for the sake of between £600-£1300 (depending on property and complexity), it is better to let someone else do the work which allows you to concentrate on other things.

Land Registry

The Land Registry records all purchases of land in England and Wales and is open to the public (inspection of records, called a property search). The registered title to any particular piece of land or property will carry with it a description and include the name of owner, mortgage, rights over other persons land and any other rights. There is a small charge for inspection. A lot of solicitors have direct links and can carry out searches very quickly. Not all properties are registered although it is now a duty to register all transactions. (See chapter 6, conveyancing)

Energy Performance Certificates (EPC's)

EPC's are compulsory. An EPC surveyor will assess the property and looks at all the ways a house or flat can waste heat, such as inadequate loft insulation, lack of cavity wall insulation, draughts and obsolete boilers. After the assessment they will award a rating from A (as good as it gets) to G (terrible). The document also includes information and advice on how to improve matters, such as lagging the water tank or installing double-glazing. An EPC will cost between £120-130 and will be valid for ten years. Improvements made while the certificate is in force will not need a new survey. However, watch out for companies that offer them for higher prices. Always search around.

Structural surveys

The basic structural survey is the homebuyers survey and valuation which is normally carried out by the building society or other lender. This will cost you between £250-£500 and is not really an in-depth survey, merely allowing the lender to see whether they should lend or not, and how much they should lend. Sometimes, lenders keep what they refer to as a retention, which means that they will not forward the full value (less deposit) until certain defined works have been carried out. If you want to go further than a homebuyers report then you will have to instruct a firm of surveyors who have several survey types, depending on how far you want to go and how much you want to spend. the average price for one of these is around £300.

A word of caution. Many people go rushing headlong into buying a flat or house. They are usually exhilarated and wish to complete their purchase fairly quickly in order to establish their new home. If you stop and think about this, it is complete folly and can prove very expensive later. A house or flat is a commodity, like other commodities, except that it is usually a lot more expensive. A lot can be wrong with the commodity that you have purchased which is not immediately obvious. Only after you have completed the deal and paid over the odds for your purchase do you begin to regret what you have done.

The true price of a property is not what the estate agent is asking, certainly not what the seller is asking. The true market price is the difference between what a property in good condition is being sold at and your property minus cost of works to bring it up to that value. Therefore, if you have any doubts whatsoever, and if you can afford it get a detailed survey of the property you are proposing to buy and get the works required costed out.

When negotiating, this survey is an essential tool in order to arrive at an accurate and fair price. Do not rest faith in others, particularly when you alone stand to lose. One further word of caution. As stated, a lot of problems with property cannot be seen. A structural survey will highlight those. In some cases it may not be wise to proceed at all.

Mortgage fees

Mortgage indemnity insurance.

This is a one-off payment if you are arranging a mortgage over 70-80% of lenders valuation. This represents insurance taken out by the lender in case the purchaser defaults on payments, in which case the lender will sell the property to reclaim the loan. It is to protect the mortgage lender not the buyer. The cost of the insurance varies depending on how much you borrow. A 90% mortgage on a £60,000 property will cost between £300-600. For a 100% mortgage it is usually much higher. You have to ask yourself, if you are paying up to £2,000 for this kind of insurance on a 100% mortgage, is it not better to try to raise the money to put down a bigger deposit. Always think about the relative economics. A lot of money is made by a lot of people in house buying and selling. The loser is usually the buyer or seller, not the host of middlemen. So think carefully about what you are doing.

Mortgage arrangement fees

Depending upon the type of mortgage you are considering you may have to pay an arrangement fee. You should budget for a minimum of £400.

Buildings insurance

When you have purchased your property you will need to take out buildings insurance. This covers the cost of rebuilding your home if it is damaged. It also covers the cost of subsidence, storm and flood damage, burst pipes and other water leaks and vandalism and third party damage generally. The insurance company will tell you more about elements covered. It is worth shopping around for buildings insurance as prices vary significantly. Many banks/building societies also supply buildings insurance if you arrange a mortgage with them. You shouldn't immediately take up their offer, as they are not always the most competitive. Websites such as www.confused.com can provide a range of quotes for you.

Removals

Unless you are not moving far and are considering doing it yourself, you should budget for hiring a removal firm. This will depend on how many possessions you have and how much time and money you have and also how far you are moving. Take care when choosing the removal firm. Choose one who comes recommended if possible. There are other costs too. Reconnection of telephone lines and possibly a deposit, carpets, curtains and plumbing-in washing machines. How much you pay will probably depend on how handy you are yourself. There are also smaller incidental costs such as redirecting mail by the post office. We will be discussing moving home in more depth later on in chapter 8.

Costs of moving

The table below will give you an idea of typical costs, such as solicitors fees, stamp duty, land registry fees and search fees when buying a property. The costs are based on a purchase of a typical London property. Other costs as discussed above will be extra. It has to be stressed that, apart from the stamp duty and Land Registry Fees (which should be checked) solicitor's costs and searches will vary. Searches will cost more in different areas and solicitors fees will come down.

House price	Solicitors fees (av)	Stamp duty	Land Registry	Search fees	Total fees
£150,000	£900	£1500	200	200	2800
£200,000	£900	£1500	200	200	£280
£300,000	£1000	9,000	280	235	10,515
£500,000	£1000	15,000	280	280	16,515
£750,000	1069	30,000	280	280	31,584
£1m	1372	50,000	920	235	52,527
£1.5m	1895	70,000	920	235	73050
£2m	2208	100,000	920	235	101363
£2.5m	2723	125,000	920	235	128,878
£3m	3656	150,000	920	235	154,811
£3.5m	4231	175,000	920	235	180,386
£4m	4871	£200000	920	235	206026

The process of buying a property

Having considered the basic elements of buying a property, the next step is to find the property you want. As we have discussed, this is a long and sometimes dispiriting process. Trudging around estate agents, sorting through mountains of literature, dealing with mountains of estate agents details, scouring the papers and walking the streets! However, most of us find the property we want at the end of the day. It is then that we can put in our offer. One useful way of determining the respective values of property in different areas is to visit a website set up for that purpose, www.hometrack.co.uk. This particular site collects price information from selected estate agents in different postcode areas across the country.

At the time of writing, prices are currently available for London and the southeast, the southwest, Birmingham and the Midlands and the north of England. Before you decide to look, a little research into prices and comparisons with what you can afford might be useful.

Making an offer

You should put your offer in to the estate agent or direct to the seller, depending who you are buying from. As discussed earlier, your offer should be based on sound judgement, on what the property is worth not on your desire to secure the property at any cost. A survey will help you to arrive at a schedule of works and cost. If you cannot afford to employ a surveyor from a high street firm then you should try to enlist other help. In addition, you should take a long and careful look at the house yourself, not just a cursory glance. Look at everything and try to get an idea of the likely cost to you of rectifying defects. However, I cannot stress enough the importance of getting a detailed survey.

Eventually, you will be in a position to make an offer for the property. You should base this offer on sound judgement and you should provide a rationalisation for your offer, if it is considerably lower than the asking price. You should make it clear that your offer is subject to contract and survey (if you require further examination or wish to carry out a survey after the offer).

Putting your own home on the market

Most people moving try to secure the sale of their own home before looking for a new one. If you haven't started to sell your house yet, you are advised to do so as soon as possible. You need also to arrange finance.

A lot of people have had the nightmarish experience of stepping into an estate agents and being besieged by "independent" financial advisors wishing to sell you their product. Be very careful at this stage. See "getting your mortgage" chapter 5.

Exchange of contracts

Once the buyer and seller are happy with all the details stated in the contract and your conveyancer can confirm that there are no outstanding legal queries, those conveyancing will exchange contracts. The sale is now legally binding for both parties. You should arrange the necessary insurances, buildings and contents from this moment on as you are now responsible for the property.

Buying with a friend

The 1996 Family Law Act brought in the concept of cohabiting couples having the same rights as married couples. This will apply particularly if your marriage starts to break up and you wish to ascertain property rights. However, it is wise to draw up a cohabitation contract prior to purchase which will put in writing how the property is shared and will make clear the situation after break-up. The cohabitation contract can include any conditions you wish and is drawn up usually by a solicitor. There are standard forms for cohabitation agreements which can include financial arrangements stating who pays for the mortgage, who can call for a sale, mutual wills, and who pays for and owns possessions. You can obtain a leaflet concerning this from a Citizens Advice Bureau or from a solicitor.

Completing a purchase

This is the final day of the sale and normally takes place around ten days after Exchange. Exchange and completion can take place on the same day if necessary but this is unusual. On day of completion, you are entitled to vacant possession and will receive the keys. See chapter seven for more details on the conveyancing process.

Buying a property in an auction

Property can be purchased in an auction. A small amount are sold in this way. Usually properties sold at auction are either unusual or difficult to put a price on or are repossessions. Auction lists can be obtained from larger estate agents or are advertised in papers. The Estates Gazette, published by the Royal Institute of Chartered Surveyors give details of auctions in each publication. Normally, this magazine is available to subscribers only although it can be ordered through a newsagent.

Preparing for auction

Because the auction is the final step of the sale, you should have any conveyancing carried out and your mortgage arranged. You will probably need to sell your old home. With this in mind it is a quick way of finding a property if you need to move quite quickly. However, it is likely that your choice of property may be limited and you will need to work on it. Many properties at auction are sub-standard, this is why they are there in the first place.

You should always do the following:

- Ask for the package compiled by the auctioneer. It will include full details of the property and the memorandum of agreement which is equivalent to the contract.
- View the house
- Organise a conveyancer and instruct him to carry out searches and arrange surveys
- If you like the property, set yourself a price limit to bid to, and arrange a mortgage.

Buying before auction

If the sales details quote "unless previously sold" the seller may be prepared to accept offers before the auction, but he will still accept a fast sale and you will be signing an auction contract. You will need to arrange conveyancing and finance very quickly.

If you are buying at the auction itself, you should remember that the fall of the hammer on your bid is equivalent to the exchange of contracts as for a private sale. You have made a legal arrangement and you will be expected to pay 10-15% deposit on the spot with the remainder of the payment within 28 days.

At the auction

If you are doubtful about your own ability then you can appoint a professional to act on your behalf although they will obviously charge for their services. The seller may be selling subject to a reserve price. If this is the case, it is normally stated in the particulars. The actual figure is not usually disclosed but if the auctioneer states something like "I am going to sell this property today" it is an indication that the reserve price has been reached.

Sale by tender

As an alternative to auction, sale by tender is like a blind auction; you don't know what the other potential buyers are offering. A form of tender is included in the sales details and sometimes sets out the contract details. Always check these details with your conveyancer, because often you cannot pull out after the offer is accepted. Buyers put their offers in an envelope, sometimes with a 10% deposit. These must be received by the seller's agent at a specified date, at which time the seller will accept one of the offers. Sale by tender is sometimes used when there have been two or three offers at similar prices.

House swapping

House swapping is an unorthodox but cost effective way of obtaining the property that you are looking for. It is a very efficient way of buying a property. Essentially, you find the property that you want and the seller moves into your house. There is no chain because you are cutting out other buyers. Obviously, the biggest problem is finding someone that you want to swap with and who wants to swap with you. In practice, the estate agent should be the ideal key player in any swap arrangement. They have a large number of people on their books and who have provided details of their requirements. However, this way of operating seems to be beyond all but the most enterprising estate agencies. In practice, most swaps happen through coincidence.

Saving money through swapping homes

There is a significant saving to be made by swapping homes. If you are the one trading down, for example you have a home worth £275,000 and you want to swap it for a flat worth £150,000, the owner of the flat will be paying for your house with part cash part property. As far as HMRC is concerned this is not a sale on which you would pay stamp duty, but a transfer on which you would pay a notional sum of just £5. However, in this particular type of transaction solicitors must draw up the deal as a single contract with the more expensive property paid partly in kind and partly in cash. You can also save on estate agents fees if you find your swap independently.

Now read the key points from Chapter 3.

Key Points From Chapter Three

1 Give careful thought to all the costs of buying property.

2 Some banks lend up to 95% of the purchase price of a property. However, in these straitened times banks are reluctant to lend too much. The more that you lend the more that it costs.

3 If the house or flat costs over £125,000 stamp duty will be payable.

4 You should consider very carefully the need for a full structural survey when buying a property.

5 Always bargain, never offer the asking price.

4

More About Mortgages

Most people purchasing a property will need a mortgage. There are many products on the market and deposits are not always required. However, it is crucial that you are in possession of all the facts when making a decision about a mortgage.

Financial advisers will give you plenty of advice but not always the best advice. Sometimes it is better to go to the lender direct. Before you talk to lenders, work out what your priorities are, such as tax advantage, early repayment and so on. Make sure that you are aware of the costs of life cover.

Lenders-Banks and building societies

There is little or no difference between the mortgages offered by banks and building societies. Because banks borrow against the wholesale money markets, the interest rate they charge to borrowers will fluctuate (unless fixed) as and when their base rate changes. Building societies however, which will rely more heavily on their savers deposits to fund their lending, may adjust the interest rate charged for variable mortgages only once a year. This may be a benefit or disadvantage, depending on whether rates are going up or down.

Centralised lenders

Centralised lenders borrow from the money markets to fund their lending and have no need for the branch network operated by banks and building societies. Centralised lenders, which came to the fore during the 1980s, particularly the house price boom, have been criticised for being quick to implement increases but slow to implement decreases, through rate reductions. This is, simply, because they exist to make profit. Therefore, you should be cautious indeed before embarking on a mortgage with lenders of this kind.

Brokers and "independent" financial advisors

Brokers act as intermediaries between potential borrowers and mortgage providers. If they are "tied" agents they can only advise on the products of one bank, insurance company or building society. If they are independent they should, technically, advise and recommend on every product in the market place.

A word of warning. It is up to you to ask detailed questions about any product a broker offers you. You should ask if they will receive a fee or commission, (the situation regarding fees and commissions to financial advisors has changed since 2013 and financial advisors now have to be more transparent) or both for any sale they arrange for you. Many brokers sell unsuitable products because they receive healthy commissions. In the 1980s it became impossible to enter an estate agents without being forced to enter into discussions with financial advisers who were intent on selling you products which made them a lot of money. If possible, you should arrange a

48

mortgage direct with a bank and avoid so called independent brokers.

How much can you borrow?

There is a standard calculation for working out the maximum mortgage that you will be allowed. For one borrower, three times annual salary, for a joint mortgage, two or two and a half times combined. Lenders, however, will vary and some will lend more. Be very careful not to overstretch yourself. As stated, banks and building societies have tightened up their lending criteria and mortgages are hard to obtain without hefty deposits although at the time of writing, 2013, the criteria is becoming a bit more relaxed in an attempt to ease up the logjam caused since the onset of the credit crunch. It really is a case of shopping around for the best deal..

Having said that, the Financial Services Authority is introducing tough new rules to ensure that no one can borrow more than they can afford to repay. These rules represent a further tightening up after the fiasco of the last ten years which has ultimately led to the present crisis. Under the new rules, interest only mortgages will only be offered to people with a firm and clear repayment plan, rather than simply relying on the rise in house prices to cover repayment of the capital. Lenders will also have to take account of future interest rate increases on repayment costs.

Deposits

Most banks and building societies used to lend 95% maximum,

some more than that. However, for now those days are largely over. Lenders will usually want higher deposits. The best source of information for reputable lenders is in the weekend newspapers. However, still, the more that you put down the better deal that you are likely to get from the lender.

Joint mortgages

If you want a joint mortgage, as for any other shared loan you and your partner have a shared responsibility for ensuring that the necessary repayments are made. If something happens to one partner then the other has total responsibility for the loan.

Main types of mortgage
Endowment

With this type of mortgage, you have to take out an endowment insurance policy which is then used to pay off the mortgage loan in a lump sum at the end of the term.

There are a number of different types designed to achieve the same end:

- Low cost with profits. This is the usual sort of endowment, guaranteeing to pay back part of the loan only. However, because bonuses are likely to be added, it is usually enough to pay off the loan in full;
- Unit linked endowment. With this, the monthly premiums are used to buy units in investment funds. The drawback is

that there is no guarantee how much the policy will be worth on maturity, since this depends on how well the investments have performed.

A word of warning. Endowment products were pushed heavily by financial brokers. There was an obsession with them in the 1980's. This is because they earn big commission for those people that sell them. Like a lot of salespeople, motivated by greed, some advisers failed to reveal the down side. This is:

-Endowments are investment linked and there is no guarantee that they will have matured sufficiently at the end of the term to repay the mortgage. This leaves you in a mess. A repayment mortgage will definitely have paid off the mortgage at the end of the term. If you change your mortgage and decide that you do not wish to continue with an endowment mortgage, and so cash in the policy early you will almost certainly get a poor return unless it is close to maturity. In the early years of the policy, most of your payments will go towards administration and commission (a fact that your broker does not always reveal). The alternative in these circumstances is to maintain the endowment until it matures, treating it as a stand-alone investment which will, hopefully, make you some money eventually.

Repayment mortgages

This mortgage, where the borrower makes regular repayments to pay the mortgage off over the term is a fairly safe bet. However, if you plan to move house every five years then this will not necessarily be the best mortgage for you. With a repayment mortgage, you pay interest every month but only a small proportion of the capital, particularly in the early years of the mortgage. An endowment mortgage, while more risky, could be better for you under these circumstances, since you can transfer the plan from property to property, while it can, hopefully, grow steadily as it matures.

Pension mortgages

Similar to the other products except that the payments go into a personal pension plan with the remainder after paying the mortgage forming the basis of a pension. The same characteristics apply as to the others.

Interest only mortgage

The borrower pays interest only on the loan, and decides how he or she will pay the loan off at the end. The lender will want to know this too, particularly in the light of the new rules being introduced, mentioned above.

Mixed mortgages

A new development is that one or two lenders now allow borrowers to mix a combination of mortgages in one deal, customising the mortgage to suit each individual.

Foreign currency mortgages

Some foreign banks offer short-term mortgages in the foreign currency of that bank. Their lending criteria can be much more relaxed than trying to borrow from a British lender. The advantage of this sort of mortgage depends on currency fluctuations. If the pound is stable or rises, the borrower benefits. If the pound drops, the borrower will have to pay more. These types of home loans should be left to more sophisticated investors as there is the potential to get into trouble unless you have a clear grasp on the implications of such a mortgage.

Cashbacks

You probably saw the adverts offering large sums of cashback if you took a particular product. If you read the small print, unless you took the highest mortgage available with the highest deposit then you would not get anywhere near such a sum. This mortgage was typical of the many mortgages on offer in the pre-credit crunch times. You would be very hard pushed to see such an offer now.

What to do if you feel that you have been given wrong advice

The mortgage lending market is very complicated and many people have suffered at the hands of financial advisors and others who have given incorrect advice. Mortgage regulation has not been very tight. However, the basic framework is as follows:

- Sales of mortgage linked investments like endowments or pensions are regulated by the Financial Services Authority. Anyone selling investments must be qualified and registered and must be able to clearly demonstrate that the policy that they have recommended is suitable. All registered individuals and firms are inspected by regulators and can be fined or expelled from the industry if guilty of wrongly selling products.

- By contrast, information on mortgages is currently regulated by the industry only, voluntarily, under a code of mortgage practice sponsored by the Council of Mortgage Lenders. Although most of the big players are signed up to the code there are still some who are not. Check first before taking advice.

How to complain

- Complain first to the company that sold you the product, going through its internal complaints procedure.
- If you are unhappy with the firm's decision, approach the relevant complaints body. For mortgage advisors employed directly by lenders, or complaints about lenders generally, contact the Financial Ombudsman Service on 0800 453 0267 or www.financial-ombudsman.org.uk
- For mortgage lenders which are not building societies or banks but which are signed up to the mortgage code, the Chartered Institute of Arbitrators 020 7421 7444 www.arbitrators.org will assist.
- If your complaint is about a mortgage broker, contact the Chartered Institute of Arbitrators which may be able to help if the firm is registered under the code.
- Complaints about endowments, pensions and other investments is handled by the Financial Services Authority 0800 606 9966 www.fsa.gov.org and are dealt with by the financial ombudsman Service.

The most common complaint is to do with endowments. A lot of people bought products which they came to regret. They are a major source of profit to the provider-and all those in between-but the person left holding the problem is the consumer.

If you believe that you have been given bad advice about anything to do with the insurance or investment side of a product then you should approach the Financial Services Authority.

The Building Societies Association www.bsa.org.uk or the British Bankers Association www.bba.org.uk have free publications that should help you. In addition, the Consumers Association, "Which" runs regular articles on mortgages. Remember - always ask questions. Never rush into anything. Always take advice if you are uncertain. Banks and building societies themselves are usually a better source, a safer source than individual advisers.

Borrowing and the internet

Almost all lenders have their own sites and many operate internet only loans with keener rates than those available on the high street. But there are also growing numbers of mortgage broker sites, offering mortgage calculators so that you can work out how much you can afford to borrow and how much the true cost of your loan will be. The following are a selection of independent sites:

www.moneysupermarket.co.uk
This is an online mortgage broker with a choice of over 4000 variable, fixed rate, capped and discounted mortgages as well as more

specialist loans for right to buy, buy to let and self build property, also self certification loans.

www.moneynet.co.uk
This is an independent on line mortgage broker, offering mortgages from over 100 lenders. Again, as with all these sites it will provide a clear and comprehensive picture of mortgages available and is easy to use, just follow the instructions.

www.moneyextra.co.uk
An independent financial advisor with access to over 4500 products including all kinds of mortgages for all types of client.

Now read the Key Points from Chapter Four overleaf.

Key Points From Chapter Four

1 There are many mortgage products on the market. Choose carefully. Understand advice- make sure all is clear.

2 The more you borrow, the more you pay at the outset and over the term.

3 If you are given wrong advice or feel aggrieved in any way there are mechanisms for complaint.

5

Selling Your Home

Estate agents

Ask for quotes from at least three agents before instructing one or more of them. The fee is normally based on the selling price of the house and is between 1 - 3 per cent of the final selling price. However, VAT (currently 20%) will be added on to this. The next chapter on conveyancing gives an idea of the processes involved once a buyer is found.

DIY Selling

If you want to save the cost of instructing an agent to sell your house, you could try to sell it yourself. Around 4 - 5% of homes in the UK are sold privately. There are a number of useful guides which are dedicated to this subject. One site worth visiting is uknetguide.co.uk. Another site is www.privatehousesearch.com.

Basically, selling properties over the internet is becoming more common, not least because it saves the seller expensive estate agents fees. See useful websites and addresses for more information about these sites.

Setting the price if selling yourself

You need to see how much similar properties are sold for in the area. If this proves difficult, get a professional valuation. See Yellow Pages under Surveyors or Valuers or contact the Royal Institution of Chartered Surveyors. A valuation report will only value and will not assess structural soundness. A survey is needed for that. Put together the sales particulars in the same way that an estate agent would. It is advisable to put a disclaimer on these details such as "these particulars are believed to be accurate and are set out as a general outline only for the guidance of interested buyers. They do not constitute, nor constitute parts of, an offer or contract.

There are a number of ways you can advertise your property. Local papers will advertise for you and also there are free ad papers. In addition, there are a number of companies with a computerised sales network who will charge you a flat fee for advertising. Be accurate with the details - you may leave yourself open to damages through misrepresentation. If an offer is made to you then you should then hand matters over to your solicitor.

As discussed, some sellers handle their own conveyancing lock stock and barrel. This includes the legal side. However, this book cannot advise you on legal conveyancing. That is a separate matter. Suffice to say that it follows a standard format. It is easier, in the light of the reduced prices available to appoint a solicitor to do this side for you.

Selling by auction
Selling by auction can be a fast way to sell your house so you should

ideally have made provision for new accommodation and storage for furniture if necessary. A date for completion is set before the auction, usually four weeks after. This is included in the selling guide. Properties are usually sold by auction in order to obtain the highest market price. An auction is also a good method if it is otherwise difficult to put a value on a property, for example if the property is unusual, as the market finds the best price.

The cost of selling by auction

Auctioneers fees are along the lines of those charged by estate agents - in the region of 1-3 per cent, but on top of this you will have to pay the preparation costs. The auctioneer will prepare a brochure and probably special advertising which you will be expected to pay for. A solicitor will be needed to carry out the legal work for you. You should remember that you will have to pay auction costs even if the property does not sell.

The aim of the auction is obviously to exceed the asking price but if you do not even reach the reserve price you can still sell privately to an interested party, possibly immediately after the auction.

If the auction is successful the auctioneer signs the contract on your behalf and receives the 10% deposit. The remaining balance is usually required within 28 days, but this detail should be specified in the contract drawn up beforehand. Earlier we saw a table giving typical costs of buying a house in London. The table below gives typical costs of the sale of a property.

Typical costs of selling a property.

House price	Solicitors fees	Estate agents fees	Total fees
£150,000	620	2,436	3,056
£200,000	652	3,276	3,928
£300,000	722	4,954	5,676
£500,000	852	8,052	8,904
£750,000	1,004	11,987	12,991
£1m	1,312	15,714	17,026
£1.5m	1,804	23,503	25,307
£2m	2,143	31,042	33,185
£2.5m	2,578	38,816	41,394
£3m	3,502	46,627	50,129
£3.5m	4,088	54,097	58,185
£4m	4,675	60,604	65,279

Now read the key Points from Chapter five overleaf.

Key points from Chapter Five

- Ask for quotes from at least three agents before agreeing to sell

- You could try to sell your property yourself. Internet selling is becoming more popular

- It is important to get an accurate valuation before selling

- Selling by auction is one route of sale if your property is proving hard to sell

6

Conveyancing a Property

Conveyancing, or the practice of conveyancing, is about how to transfer the ownership of land and property from one person or organisation to another. Land and property can include freehold property, leasehold property (residential) or can include business leases. *Essentially, the process of conveyancing lays down clear procedures for the conveyancer and also sets out each party's position during the sale or acquisition.*

Before understanding the process of conveyancing, however, it is essential to understand something about the legal forms of ownership of property.

Legal ownership of property

There are two main forms of legal ownership of property in Great Britain. If you are about to embark on the sale or acquisition of a house or flat (or business) then you will be dealing in the main with either freehold or leasehold property. It is very rare indeed to find other forms of ownership, although the government has introduced a form of ownership called 'common hold' that in essence creates the freehold ownership of flats, with common responsibility for communal areas.

Freehold property

In general, if you own the freehold of a house or a piece of land, then you will be the outright owner with no fixed period of time and no one else to answer to (with the exception of statutory authorities).

There may be registered restrictions on title, which will be discussed later. The property will probably be subject to a mortgage so the only other overriding interest will be that of the bank or the building society. The responsibility for repairs and maintenance and general upkeep will be the freeholders. The law can intervene if certain standards are not maintained.

The deed to your house will be known as the "freehold transfer document" which will contain any rights and obligations. Usually, the transfer document will list any "encumbrances" (restrictions) on the use of the land, such as rights of way of other parties, sales restrictions etc. The deeds to your home are the most important documentation. As we will see later, without deeds and historical data, such as the root of title, it can be rather complicated selling property. This is why the system of land registration in use in this country has greatly simplified property transactions. *Any person owning freehold property is free to create another interest in land, such as a lease or a weekly or monthly tenancy, subject to any restrictions the transfer may contain.*

Leasehold property

If a person lives in a property owned by someone else and has an agreement for a period of time, usually a long period, over 21 years and up to 99 years or 125 years, in some cases 999 years, then they are a leaseholder. The conveyancing of leasehold property is, potentially, far more problematic than freehold property, particularly when the flat is in a block with a number of units. The lease is a contract between landlord and tenant which lays down the rights and obligations of both parties and should be read thoroughly by both the leaseholder and, in particular, the conveyancer. Once signed then the purchaser is bound by all the clauses in the contract. It is worth taking a little time looking at the nature of a lease before discussing the rather more complex process of conveyancing. Again, it has to be stated that it is of the utmost importance that both the purchaser and the vendor understand the nature of a lease.

The lease-Preamble

The start of a lease is called the preamble. This defines the landlord and purchaser and also the nature of the property in question (the demise). It will also detail the remaining period of the lease.

Leaseholders covenants

Covenants are best understood as obligations and responsibilities. Leaseholder's covenants are therefore a list of things that leaseholders should do, such as pay their service charges and keep the interior of the dwelling in good repair and not to, for example, alter the structure. The landlord's covenants will set out the obligations of the landlord, which is usually to maintain the structure and exterior of the block, light common parts etc.

One unifying theme of all leasehold property is that, notwithstanding the landlord's responsibilities, it is the leaseholder who will pay for everything out of a service charge.

Leases will make detailed provisions for the setting, managing and charging of service charges, which should include a section on accounting. All landlords of leaseholders are accountable under the Landlord and Tenant Act 1985, as amended. These Acts will regulate the way a landlord treats a leaseholder in the charging and accounting of service charges.

In addition, the 1996 Housing Act, as amended by the 2002 Commonhold and Leasehold Reform Act has provided further legislation protecting leaseholders by introducing the right of leaseholders to go to Leasehold Valuation Tribunals if they are unhappy with levels and management of charges and also to carry out audits of charges. It is vital that, when buying a leasehold property that you read the lease. Leases tend to be different from each other and nothing can be assumed. When you buy a property, ensure that the person selling has paid all debts and has contributed to some form of "sinking fund" whereby provision has been built up for major repairs in the future. Make sure that you will not be landed with big bills after moving in and that, if you are, there is money to deal with them. After a lease has been signed then there is little or no recourse to recoup any money owed.

These are all the finer points of leases and the conveyancer has to be very vigilant. In particular read the schedules to the lease as these sometimes contain rather more detail.

One of the main differences between leasehold and freehold property is that the lease is a long tenancy agreement which contains provisions which give the landlord rather a lot of power to manage (or mismanage) and it is always a possibility that a leaseholder can be forced to give up his or her home in the event of non compliance with the terms of the lease. This is known as forfeiture.

Under legislation referred to earlier, a new 'no fault right to manage' has been introduced. This enables leaseholders who are unhappy with the management of their property, to take over the management with relative ease. The Act applies to most landlords, with the exception of Local Authorities. These powers go a long way to curb the excesses or inefficiencies of numerous landlords and provide more control and greater security for leaseholders.

Check points

There are key areas of a lease that should be checked when purchasing. Some have already been discussed.

- What is the term left on the lease?
- Is the preamble clear, i.e. is the area which details landlord, tenant and demised (sold) premises, clear?
- Is the lease assignable- i.e. can you pass on the lease without landlords permission or does it need surrendering at sale or a license to assign?
- What is the ground rent and how frequently will you pay it?
- What is the level of service charge, if any, and how is it collected, apportioned, managed and accounted for?

- What are the general restrictions in the lease, can you have pets for example, can you park cars and do you have a designated space?
- What are the respective repairing obligations? As we have seen, the leaseholder will pay anyway but the landlord and leaseholder will hold respective responsibilities. This is an important point because occasionally, there is no stated responsibility for upkeep and the environment deteriorates as a consequence, diminishing the value of the property.

Two systems of conveyancing

After gaining an understanding of the nature of the interest in land that you are buying, it is absolutely essential to understand the two systems of conveyancing property in existence, as this will determine, not so much the procedure because the initial basic steps in conveyancing, such as carrying out searches, are common to both forms of land, registered and unregistered, but the way you go about the process and the final registration.

Registered and unregistered land

In England and Wales the method of conveyancing to be used in each particular transaction very much depends on whether the land is *registered* or *unregistered* land. If the title, or proof of ownership, of land and property has been registered under the Land Registration Acts 1925-86 then the Land Registry (see below) will be able to furnish the would-be conveyancer with such documentation as is required to establish ownership, third party rights etc. If the land has not been registered then proof of ownership of the land in question must be traced through the title deeds.

Registered land

As more and more conveyancing is falling within the remit of the Land Registry, because it is compulsory to register land throughout England and Wales, it is worth outlining this system briefly at this stage.

The Land Registration Acts of 1925 established the Land Registry (HM Land Registry). The Land Registry is a department of the Civil Service, at its head is the Chief Land Registrar. All applications to the Land Registry must be made within the district in question.

There is a specific terminology in use within conveyancing, particularly within the land registry:

a) *a piece of land*, or parcel of land is known as a *registered title*
b) the owner of land is referred to as the *registered proprietor*
c) a conveyance of registered land is called *a transfer*
d) a transaction involving registered land is known as *a dealing*

The main difference between the two types of conveyancing *registered* and *unregistered* concerns what is known *as proof of title*. In the case of land that is unregistered the owner will prove title by showing the would-be purchaser the documentary evidence which shows how he or she came to own the land and property. In the case of registered land the owner has to show simply that he or she is registered at the Land Registry as the registered proprietor. Proof of registration is proof of ownership, which is unequivocal. In registered land the documents proving ownership are replaced by the fact of registration. Each separate title or ownership of land has a title number, which the Land Registry uses to trace ownership, or confirm ownership. The description of each title on the register is identified by the *title number,* described by reference to the filed plan (indicating limits and extent of ownership). With registered conveyancing the Land Registry keeps the register of title and file plan and title. The owner (proprietor) is issued with a Land Certificate. If the land in question is subject to a mortgage then the mortgagee is issued with a Land Certificate.

Production of the Land Certificate

With registered land, whenever there is a sale, or disposition, then the Land Certificate must be produced to the Land Registry in the appropriate district. If proved that a Certificate is lost or destroyed then a new one can be issued by the Land Registry.

The key steps in the process of conveyancing property

Before the buyer exchanges contracts on a property, whether registered or unregistered, and then completes the purchase a number of searches are always carried out. These are:

Enquiry's before contract
Local land charges search
Enquiry's of the local authority
Index map search

The above searches will now be carried out by the seller, or by the agent acting for the seller, prior to marketing the property through the HIP.

These are the most essential and common searches.

Making enquiry's before contract

These are enquiry's to the seller, or the Vendor of the property and are aimed at revealing certain facts about the property that the seller has no legal obligation to disclose to the buyer. There are certain matters, which are always raised. These are:

a) Whether there are any existing boundary disputes
b) What services are supplied to the property, whether electricity, gas or other
c) Any easements or covenants in the lease. These are stipulations in the lease, which give other certain rights, such as rights of way.
d) Any guarantees in existence
Planning considerations
a) Adverse rights affecting the property
b) Any fixtures and fittings
c) Whether there has been any breach of restriction affecting the property

If the property is newly built, information will be required concerning any outstanding works or future guarantees of remedying defects. Where a property is leasehold, information will be required about the lessor.

Registered conveyancers will use a standard form to raise these enquiry's, so that the initial search is exhaustive. As part of the move towards openness in the process of buying and selling property, and also an attempt to speed up the process of sale, the Law Society has introduced new forms which the solicitor, or buyer if carrying out his or her own conveyancing, is being encouraged to use. These are Seller's Property Information Forms relating to freehold and leasehold property, that the seller and solicitor will respectively fill in, a form relating to fixtures, fittings and contents and a form relating to complete information and requisitions on title. These forms can be obtained from a legal stationers, such as Oyez and have the pre-fix Prop 1-7.

If a conveyancer is being used then it is advisable to ask whether or not they are using these newly introduced forms. The main point is that you should think long and hard about the type of questions that should be raised. The vendor does not have to answer the questions, but beware a vendor who refuses to disclose answers. Answers given by the vendor do not form part of the subsequent contract and therefore cannot be used against that person in the event of future problems. However, the Misrepresentations Act of 1976 could be evoked if a deliberate misrepresentation has caused problems.

Local land charges search

The Local Land Charges Act 1975 requires District Councils, London Borough Councils and the City of London Corporation to maintain a Local Land Charges Registry for the area. Local land charges can be divided into two areas:

a) Financial charges on the land for work carried out by the local authority
b) restrictions on the use of land

The register is further divided into twelve parts:

a) general financial charges
b) specific financial charges
c) planning charges
d) miscellaneous charges and provisions
e) charges for improvements of ways over fenland
f) land compensation charges
g) new town charges
h) civil aviation charges
i) open cast coal mining charges
j) listed buildings charges
k) light obstruction notices
l) drainage scheme charges

All charges are enforceable by the local authority except g and i, which are enforced by statutory bodies and private individuals generally. A buyer should search in all parts of this particular register and this can be done by a personal or official search. A personal search, as the name suggests, involves the individual or their agent attending at the local authority office and, on paying the relevant fee, personally searching the register. The charges are registered against the land concerned and not against the owner. The official search is the one most favored because, in the event of missing a vital piece of information the chances of compensation are far higher than with a personal search. With the official search a requisition for a search and for an official certificate of search is sent to the Registrar of Local Land Charges for the area within which the land is situated. There is a fee and the search is carried out by the Registrars staff, which results in a certificate being sent to the person making the request, which clearly outlines any charges. The Registrar may require a plan of the land as well as the postal address. Separate searches are made of each parcel of land being purchased.

Local authority searches

There is a standard form in use for these particular types of searches. This is known as "Con 29 England and Wales" Revised April 2000, with the format of the form differing slightly for inner London boroughs. Any of the forms in the process can be obtained from legal stationers.

The standard forms in use contain a statement to the effect that the local authority is not responsible for errors unless negligence is proved. Many of the enquiries relate specifically to planning matters, whilst other elements of the search are concerned about roads and whether they are adopted and whether there are likely to be any costs falling onto property owners.

We will be considering planning matters concerning the individual property a little later. Other enquiry's relate to possible construction of new roads which may affect the property, the location of sewers and pipes and whether the property is in an area of compulsory registration of title, a smoke control area or slum clearance area. The form used is so constructed that part 2 of the form contains questions, which must be initialled by the purchaser before they are answered. Again these questions cover planning and other matters. Other enquiry's can be asked by the individual, which are answered at the authorities discretion. In addition to the above, which are the major searches, there are others that the conveyancer has to be aware of. These are as follows:

Searches in the Index map and parcels index of the Land register

If the land has been registered the title will be disclosed and whether it is registered leasehold or freehold. Registered rent charges are also disclosed by the search. (See chapter 7.)

Commons Registration Act (1965) search

This act imposes a duty on County Councils to keep a register relating to village greens and common land and interests over them, such as right of way.

Coal mining search

The request for this search if relevant, is designed to reveal the whereabouts of mineshafts and should be sent to the local Area Coal Board office, or its equivalent. The search will disclose past workings and any subsidence, proposed future workings and the proximity of opencast workings. It is usually well known if there is a problem, or potential problem with coal mining in an area and this search is essential if that is the case.

Other enquiry's

There are a number of other bodies from which it might be appropriate to request a search. These include British Rail, statutory undertakers such as electricity and gas boards, planning authorities generally, rent assessment committees and so on. These will only usually be necessary if there is a direct link between the property being purchased and a particular circumstance within an area or property.

Planning matters relating to specific properties

It is obviously very necessary to determine whether or not any illegal alterations have been carried out to the property you wish to purchase, before reaching the point of exchange of contracts. This is to ensure that the vendor has complied with relevant planning legislation, if any material changes have been made, and that you will not be required at a later date to carry out remedial work. The Local Authority maintains a register of planning applications relating to properties within their boundaries. In addition, the register will also reveal any planning enforcement notices in force against a particular property.

Questions such as these, and also any questions relating to the effect of Structure or Local plans, (specific plans relating to local and borough wide plans for the future) should be made in writing to the local authority or an individual search can be carried out. Usually they are carried out if there is any suspicion that planning regulations may have been breached.

In addition, there may be other considerations, such as whether the building is listed or whether tree preservation orders relating to trees within the cartilage of the property are in force. It is certainly essential to know about these. It is highly recommended that all of these searches are carried out and completed before contracts are exchanged.

The contract for sale

As with many other transactions, a sale of land is effected through a contract. However, a contract, which deals with the sale of land, is governed by the requirements of the Law of Property (miscellaneous provisions) Act 1989, the equitable doctrine of specific performance and the duty of the vendor to provide title to the property. The Law of Property Act (Miscellaneous provisions) 1988 provides that contracts dealing with the sale of land after 26th September 1989 must be in writing. The contract must contain all the terms and agreements to which the respective parties to the transaction have agreed. The provisions of the Act do not apply to sales at a public auction, contracts to grant a short lease and contracts regulated under the Financial Services Act 1986. If the person purchasing is doing so through an agent then the agent must have authority to act on behalf of the purchaser. Examples of agents are auctioneers and solicitors, also estate agents. If the phrase "subject to contract" is used in a sale then the intention of both parties to the contract is that neither are contractually bound until a formal contract has been agreed by the parties, signed and exchanged. Therefore, the words "subject to contract" are a protective device, although it is not good to depend on the use of these words throughout a transaction

Procedures in the formation of contract

The vendor's solicitor will usually draw up an initial contract of sale. This is because only this person has access to all the necessary initial documents to begin to effect a contract. The draft contract is prepared in two parts and sent to the purchaser's solicitor (if using a solicitor), the other side will approve or amend the contract as necessary. Both sides must agree to any proposed amendments. After agreement has been reached, the vendor's solicitor will retain one copy of the contract and send the other copy to the solicitor or person acting for the other side.

The next stage is for the vendors solicitor to engross (sign and formalise) the contract in two parts. Both parts are then sent to the purchaser's solicitor or other agent who checks that they are correct then sends one part back to the vendor's solicitor.

The Contents of a contract

A contract will be in two parts, *the particulars of sale* and the *conditions of sale*. The particulars of sale give a physical description of the land and also of the interest, which is being sold. A property must be described accurately and a plan may be attached to the contract to emphasize or illustrate what is in the contract. The particulars will also outline whether the property is freehold or leasehold and what kind of lease the vendor is assigning, i.e., head lease (where vendor is owner of the freehold) or underlease, where the vendor is not.

It is very important to determine what kind of lease it is that is being assigned, indeed whether it is assignable or whether permission is needed from the landlord and it is recommended that a solicitor handle this transaction. This is because any purchaser of a lease can find his or her interest jeopardized by the nature of the lease. Where a sub-lease, or under lease is being purchased, the purchasers interest can be forfeited by the actions of the head lessee, the actions of this person being out of control of the purchaser.

Rights, such as easements and also restrictive covenants, which are for the benefit of the land, should be expressly referred to in the particulars of sale. In addition, the vendor should refer to any latent defects affecting his or her property, if known. This includes any encumbrances, which may affect the property.

Misdescription

If the property in the particulars of sale is described wrongly, i.e. there is a mis-statement of fact, such as describing leasehold as freehold land, calling an under-lease a lease or leaving out something that misleads the buyer, in other words, if the misdescription is material, then the purchaser is entitled to rescind the contract. Essentially the contract must describe what is being sold and if it does not, and the buyer is mislead then the contract is inaccurate. If the misdescription is immaterial and insubstantial, and there has been no misrepresentation then the purchaser cannot rescind the contract. However, if the misdescription has affected the purchase price of the property then the purchaser can insist on a reduction in the asking price. The purchaser should claim this compensation before completion takes place. The vendor has no right to rescind the contract if the misdescription is in the purchaser's favour, for example, the area of land sold is greater than that intended. Neither can the vendor compel the purchaser to pay an increased purchase price

Misrepresentation

Misrepresentation is an untrue statement of fact made by one party or his or her agent, which induces the other party to enter into the contract. An opinion and a statement of intention must be distinguished from a statement of fact.

There are three types of misrepresentation, fraudulent misrepresentation, negligent misrepresentation and innocent misrepresentation. Fraudulent misrepresentation is a false statement made knowingly or without belief in its truth, or recklessly. The innocent party may sue through the tort of negligence either before or after the contract is complete and rescind the contract. Negligent misrepresentation, although not fraudulent, is where the vendor or his or her agents cannot prove that the statement they made in relation to the contract was correct.

Remedies available are damages or rescission of the contract. Innocent misrepresentation is where the statement made was neither fraudulently or negligently but is still an untrue statement. Rescission is available for this particular type of misrepresentation. Rescission of contract generally is available under the Misrepresentation Act 1967 s 2(2).

Non-disclosure

Generally, in the law of contract, there is the principle of "caveat emptor" "let the buyer beware". In other words, it is up to the purchaser to ensure that what he or she is buying is worth the money paid for it. Earlier we talked about the importance of searches and also, particularly, the importance of the structural survey. Although the vendor has some responsibility to reveal any defects in the property it is always very advisable for the purchaser to ensure that all checks prior to purchase are carried out thoroughly.

Signing the contract

The vendors solicitor will obtain the vendors signature to the contract, when he is satisfied that the vendor can sell what he is purporting to do through the contract. The purchaser's solicitor or agent will do the same, having checked the replies to all enquiry's before contract. It is also essential to check that a mortgage offer has been made and accepted.

Exchanging contracts

Neither party to the sale is legally bound until there has been an exchange of contracts. At one time, a face to face exchange would have taken place. However, with the rapid increases in property transactions this rarely happen nowadays. Exchange by post is more common. The purchaser will post his or her part of the contract together with the appropriate cheque to cover the agreed deposit, to the purchaser's solicitor or person acting on behalf of that Person.

The purchaser's solicitor will usually insert the agreed completion date. On receiving this part of the contract the vendor will add his or her part and send this off in exchange. At this stage, both parties become bound under the contract.

A contract to convey or create an estate in land is registrable as a class C (IV) land charge, an estate contract. You should take further advice on this, as it is not current practice to do so.

Completion

The requirements concerning completion are detailed thoroughly in the general conditions of sale. Payment on completion is one such detail. Payment on completion should be by one of the following methods:
a) legal tender;
b) bankers draft;
c) an unconditional authority to release any deposit by the stakeholder
d) any other method agreed with the vendor.

At common law, completion takes place whenever the vendor wishes and payment is to be made by legal tender. Also dealt with in the general conditions is failure to complete and notices to complete. Failure to complete can cause difficulty for one of the other parties and the aggrieved party can serve notice on the other to complete by a specific date. The notice has the effect of making "time of the essence" which means that a specific date is attached to completion, after which the contract is discharged.

Return of pre-contract deposits

The vendor must return any deposit paid to the purchaser if the purchaser drops out before the exchange of contracts. This cannot be prevented and was the subject of a House of Lords (now the Supreme Court) ruling.

The position of the parties after exchange of contracts

Once a contract has been exchanged, the purchaser is the beneficial owner of the property, with the vendor owning the property on trust for the purchaser. The vendor is entitled to any rents or other profits from the land during this period, has the right to retain the property until final payments have been made and has a lien (charge/right) over the property in respect of any unpaid purchase monies.

The vendor is bound to take reasonable care of the property and should not let the property fall into disrepair or other damages to be caused during the period between exchange and completion. If completion does not take place at the allotted time and the fault is the purchasers then interest can be charged on the money due.

The purchaser, as beneficial owner of the property is entitled to any increase in the value of the land and buildings but not profits arising. The purchaser has a right of lien over the property, the same as the vendor, in respect of any part of the purchase price paid prior to completion.

Bankruptcy of the vendor

In the unfortunate event of the vendor going bankrupt in between exchange and completion, the normal principles of bankruptcy apply so that the trustee in bankruptcy steps in to the vendor's shoes. The purchaser can be compelled to complete the sale. The trustee in bankruptcy is obliged to complete the sale if the purchaser tenders the purchase money on the completion day.

Bankruptcy of the purchaser

When a purchaser is declared bankrupt in between sale and completion all of his or her property vests in the trustee in bankruptcy. In these circumstances, the vendor can keep any deposit due to him.

Death of Vendor or purchaser

The personal representatives of a deceased vendor can compel the purchaser to sell. The money is conveyed to those representatives who will hold the money in accordance with the terms of any will or in accordance with the rules relating to intestacy if there is no will.

The same position applies to the purchaser's representatives, who can be compelled by the vendor to complete the purchase and who can hold money on the purchaser's behalf.

Now read the key points from chapter 6

Key Points From Chapter 6

- Conveyancing is about the practice of transferring a property from one to another.

- There are two main types of property ownership in Britain- Freehold and leasehold

- The lease is the single most important document if buying leasehold

- There are two systems of conveyancing – registered and unregistered.

- The contract of sale must be scrutinised thoroughly before exchange and completion

7

Planning Moving Arrangements

At this stage, you will either have sold your home and /or be ready to move into a new one. The process of moving home is closely linked with the completion of the purchase of another home. That is, assuming that you are moving to another bought property. Of course, you may be moving to a rented home.

However you choose to time your move, there are certain core tasks, as follows:

- Finalise removal and storage arrangements
- Contact electricity/gas/phone/cable companies and any other relevant company to tell them your moving date
- Organise your funds so that you can transfer all remaining money needed to complete the sale into your solicitors account for him/her to pay the sellers solicitor

One main question is: do you get a removal firm or do you do it yourself?

DIY moves

This is cheaper than hiring a removal company, especially if you have a few possessions or no big items of furniture. You will also need willing and able friends. However, do not take the decision to move yourself lightly. Think carefully about the amount of furniture that you have and the fact that your house may be a particularly difficult site to move from.

Using professionals

Professionals know what they are doing and can leave you to organise all the other aspects of moving whilst they do the donkey work. This may cost you more money. However, it may be well worth it. Use a firm which is a member of the British Association of Removers (www.bar.co.uk). Members of this body have to adhere to a code of professional practice, meet minimum standards and provide emergency service and finance guarantees.

Removers can offer various levels of packing services. The most expensive option is for the remover to pack everything. The second most expensive option is for them to pack the breakable things such as glass. The cheapest way is for the removers to provide crates and for you to do your own packing.

If you are going for the professional option:

- Get two or three estimates. You can find the names of local firms through the British Association of Removers, through the yellow pages (www.yell.com) or through Thomson's Directories (www.thomweb.co.uk)
- There are a growing number of websites that include quotes from removal firms (see below)

- You should expect estimators to go through your whole property including gardens and loft
- Check whether your possessions will be covered by your household insurance policy and extend the cover if they are not
- Don't wait to exchange contracts to organise removers.

The following Websites may be useful:

www.reallymoving.com

This site was launched in 1999 and is the leading provider of online removal services. Registering on the site will get you three quotes from removers. It also covers solicitors, surveyors and others involved in the buying and selling process.

Contacting utilities

A boring but essential task is to contact all of the companies that provide you with services to tell them that you have moved. This should be done after you exchange contracts, obtaining meter readings etc. Most utilities will ask you for confirmation of your new address and moving date in writing. If you cannot face this task then use the following website:

www.iammoving.com

This site was started in 1999 by a consortium of investors and industry figures. The claim is to be the UK's first free online change of address service. You register, enter your old and new address, supply account numbers and meter readings where relevant and iammoving will send the information to the appropriate companies.

The process is quick and relatively uncomplicated.

****

8

Buying and Selling in Scotland

Scotland has it own system of law, and buying and selling a house or flat is quite a different process from doing so in England, Wales or Northern Ireland. The system generally works more quickly and there is less risk of gazumping.

Looking for property

Solicitors, property centres and offices. These are the largest source of properties available in Scotland. Often found in town centres, the property centres provide information in a similar way to estate agents outside Scotland.

Newspapers. Daily Scottish newspapers are a good source of property. Regional and local newspapers carry many details on a regular basis.

Estate agents. These offer the same service

Ownership of property in Scotland

Property in Scotland does not exist as freehold or leasehold, as in England. Instead a "feudal tenure" system exists. This means that, as in freehold, the owner has right to building and land. However, the original owner of the development still has some say over any alterations and use of the land. These feuing conditions are permanent and should be checked before purchase is considered. A new owner (feuar) can negotiate to have conditions waived, but there may be a charge for this. Further details of the system can be obtained from the lands tribunal for Scotland or your solicitor.

House prices

Property in Scotland is normally sold as "offers over" (sometimes called the upset price) the price set is usually the minimum and may not be negotiated down. This method is used where the property is likely to prove popular and to get the best price. If a quick sale is required a property may be sold as "fixed price" the seller will take the first offer at that price. If there is more than one prospective purchaser the seller may opt to set a closing date for offers. The process is then like a blind bid, with none of the buyers knowing the price anyone else is bidding. Although the seller usually accepts the highest price, this is not always the case; other factors, such as date of entry, may be taken into consideration.

The buying process-Surveys

These are carried out before a formal offer is made. In some circumstances you may end up losing money, if your offer is not accepted. There are no licensed conveyancers in Scotland. Because solicitors do all the conveyancing and are so involved in the process then they will usually arrange surveys.

Making an offer

Your interest in buying a house is relayed via your solicitor to the selling solicitor by word of mouth. It does not have any legal standing and either party may pull out. Formal offer comes by letter, through the solicitor, and will include any items such as fixtures and fittings. The letter forms part of contract of sale.

Exchange of missives

If the offer is accepted, a formal letter called qualified acceptance is returned by the sellers solicitor, confirming or amending the conditions. The entry date may need to be negotiated to suit both parties. These formal letters are referred to as missives and may go back and forth for clarification.

Missives concluded

Once all the conditions are agreed, the purchase is then legally binding for both buyer and seller. The missives are concluded by the acting solicitors: neither the buyer or the seller signs anything. There is no deposit paid in the Scottish system except if you are buying a new house from a property developer

The law states that once the missives have been concluded, the purchaser is responsible for the insurance of the property. However, it is more usual for an agreement to be made in the missives that the seller remains liable until the date of entry. The date that you would like to move is suggested in your formal offer to the seller. In this time you should be able to sell your house and complete any legal work. Before the date of entry, your solicitor will prepare what is known as a disposition to confirm the change of ownership. He will obtain from the sellers solicitor the title deeds which will be signed by the seller to agree the change of ownership. These will be handed over on the date of entry following payment of the property price.

Searches

There are two types of searches in Scotland:
Immediately prior to exchanging missives a search on the property and against the individual is made. This checks that the seller has a good title to the property and that the purchaser can grant security for the loan. In addition, a local authority search forms part of the missives. It checks that there are no proposed developments that would affect the property.

Selling a house or flat
Ways of selling your home

The majority of houses are bought and sold through solicitor offices, but you also have the options of selling through an estate agent or selling it privately yourself. Whatever option you choose, it is customary in Scotland to show prospective buyers around the house and explain the details.

DIY selling
This involves setting the price, preparing the sales details about the house, advertising it and showing people around. The advantages of

this kind of sale are that you cut out middlemen and save commission. However, you will need a solicitor for conveyancing.

Selling through an estate agent

These are normally Scottish branches of well-known chains of agents. They offer a service similar to their English counterparts. In contrast to selling through a solicitor, estate agents often encourage you to take the first offer rather than generating interest and setting a closing date. You should get quotes from agents about their charges. this will be typically around 1.5% of selling price.

Selling through a solicitor

Most property in Scotland is sold through solicitors. They provide a service similar to estate agents and have property centres displaying details of houses for sale, although there may be an extra one off charge for this depending on the area you are in. Their commission charges are often slightly cheaper than those of estate agents. It is normal practice to use the same solicitor to sell your house and carry out the legal side of the sale.

The selling process

Your solicitor or estate agent will prepare the sales particulars and discuss the selling price with you as part of their contract. Depending upon the circumstances, they will advise as to whether the house is sold as "offers above" or as "fixed price". The former is usually set slightly below the expected price to encourage buyers. If a degree of competitiveness is created you may be able to set a "closing" date which usually achieves a better selling price.

Legally you should leave all fixtures and fittings, such as carpets and curtains or kitchen equipment unless you draw up a contract which states otherwise.

The legal services of your solicitor

There are two main areas the solicitor will need to follow up to allow smooth progress of a house sale.

The title deeds will need to be examined to check that you are the true owner of the property. Scottish law includes the Matrimonial Homes (Family Protection) (Scotland) Act: even if only one spouse owns the property permission to sell must be given by the partner.

Conveyancing will involve property surveys, and local searches to check there are no proposals for developments. If you are using a solicitor to sell your house, they may offer an overall charge that covers selling and legal services.

Accepting offers

Your solicitor will inform you if anyone has shown an interest in your property. If a lot of interest is shown in your house, you could consider setting a closing date for offers. Your solicitor or estate agent should advise you whether this is a good idea. There is no point in setting a date until you are sure more than one person is likely to make a formal offer. The closing date is a specific time on a specific day that all formal offers will be assessed. You are not obliged to accept any offer if they are too low. Nor does the highest offer have to be accepted.

If you accept the highest offer, your solicitor may negotiate points concerning other conditions, such as extras included or dates, but there must be no attempt to try to raise the price offered. If you are using an estate agent, their role ends once the offer has been handed over to the solicitor.

A formal offer will include all the conditions of sale, the price, any items included, and the date of entry. Some offers are made with a time limit in which you must accept verbally, which can be as little as within 24 hours. You should seek advice from your solicitors whether to act promptly. You may be advised to hold out for a higher offer. If the purchaser is seriously interested they will not mind waiting for an acceptance.

Your solicitor will engage in the process of exchanging missives with the buyers solicitor. Missives are formal letters laying down conditions of sale and may be passed back and forth until an amicable agreement is reached. Once final missives have been exchanged the contract is legally binding for both parties, so it is important that you are familiar with all the conditions being negotiated by your solicitor through the missives. It will be too late once they have finally been changed.

Setting an entry date

The date for finalising the sale is suggested by both the seller and by the buyer in his offer. It is negotiated by both parties and a mutually agreed date is written into the missives. This is the date when the keys are handed to your solicitor, and you must move out. Although the date of entry is set by the seller, it may need to be changed to achieve a compromise which suits you and the purchaser.

Completion

Title deeds. Your buyer's solicitor will need to prepare the disposition and for this your solicitor will send the title deeds. The disposition is the document that states the change of ownership on the title deeds, and will need to be signed by you. It is handed over to the purchaser's solicitor in exchange for payment of the property on the date of settlement.

Now read the Key Points from Chapter Eight overleaf.

Key Points From Chapter 8

1 The process of buying and selling property in Scotland is quite different to that in England.

2 Property in Scotland does not exist as freehold or leasehold. Instead a Feudal tenure exists.

3 "Gazumping" is not possible in Scotland. Once an offer is made it is virtually binding.

4 Solicitors play a very important part in the process of buying and selling property in Scotland.

Chapter 9

Buying a Property Abroad

In the last 10-15 years or so, the world has shrunk considerably. Whereas not so long ago, most people, British and others, were buying property in Southern Europe, particularly France, Spain, Portugal and Italy, (with the exception of a few adventurous souls) nowadays virtually the whole of Europe is open thanks mainly to the proliferation of countries entering the European union. It is now possible to buy a property, for leisure or for investment throughout the whole of Europe and also, thanks to ever cheaper air travel, in many countries throughout the world.

Although this book is being written in the aftermath of a credit crunch, and a recession throughout Europe, due to ever increasing oil prices and banks overstretching themselves, the very fact that property prices are falling and life is getting tougher, will also mean that those with the wherewithal will take their money and go in search of properties in up and coming countries, such as Poland, the Baltic States and also countries such as Albania. Many people invest in countries where the climate is better than the UK, although just as many seem now to be investing in Eastern Europe, in search of culture rather than weather.

Other factors influencing would be investors or those in search of a second home are stable interest rates and the low costs of borrowing money. Many hitherto inaccessible countries are now literally bending over backwards to make themselves attractive to foreign investors. An influx of foreign capital, along with foreign expertise is exactly what is needed now the old shackles have been removed and membership of the EU is creating the conditions for future prosperity. The average investment in property in the new EU countries is now approaching £150,000, with lots of variations above and below that price. Whereas it was once mainly the elderly who desired that retirement home abroad, the mix of people buying abroad, for whatever reason, spans all age groups. Indeed, since property started to escalate and the cost of living generally spiraled, many people have chosen to leave the UK in search of a better life.

Many a dream has been shattered by the realties of different countries regimes covering property purchase. For sure there are estate agents now in most countries who will help guide a person through the maze. However, it has to be realised that those agents are also acting in their own interests.

Below are a few tips to ponder when thinking of buying a Property abroad.

Buying off-plan

In the UK, a growth industry, corresponding to the opening-up of the property market, has been that of property exhibitions. Every where you go or look there are now property exhibitions selling the delights of property investment in just about every country that you can think of. Many of these exhibitions will be selling properties off plan, i.e., before they are built. Clearly this is good for developers in that they have increased cash flow and guaranteed sales. The advantage for buyers, so it goes, is that by the time the property is ready the value will exceed what you paid for it. So you have an instant profit.

Before you buy a property off-plan you are required to have at least 20% deposit and also have all the necessary paperwork in place. You shouldn't forget that salespeople make hefty commissions out of those who buy off-plan and they will be using every trick in the book to ensure that they get your business. The scheme will have been heavily promoted and journalists will often be flown across to give a glowing review of the development. It is vitally important that you have knowledge of the developer, the country in which the property is being purchased and the potential pitfalls. In many cases the property that you are purchasing may not be ready for several years. Will the developer still be in business? Remember they have your money! Always do your research before committing anything-do not be swayed by heavy selling and the pressure that comes with it.

Pitfalls to watch out for

Whether you are buying for investment or for leisure you don't want to end up poorer for the experience. There are a number of factors to consider and to bear in mind when buying a property abroad:

- Never believe that because a budget airline is either planning to, or has, introduced flights to a particular country that the price of property will rise. This is not the case and many airlines will introduce and then withdraw flights if they are not proving profitable;
- Always consider the associated costs when purchasing a property, what are the maintenance costs and what are local taxes and so on. Thorough research is necessary here before committing yourself;
- In particular, understand the tax regimes of a country before

committing yourself. Some regimes are particularly harsh and you could also find yourself in a double tax situation, such as when/ if you choose to rent a property out.

- If you are hoping to rent a property out once purchased make sure that you do extensive research beforehand. Many developers are offering so called 'guaranteed rentals' to those who purchased property. Why should they do this if what they are offering is greater than the normal return? This is because, notwithstanding whether they can rent it for this guaranteed rental, the developer has already factored this rental into the purchase price. Another gimmick!

- What are the conditions for selling the property. This is very important. Look for signs of over development in a country, as has happened in Bulgaria and has certainly happened in Spain.

- What are the general conditions for obtaining a reasonable price for renovation in a country and what is the likelihood of getting ripped off. There are numerous websites which invite people to give their opinions of buying a property in a particular country and also offer the benefit of hindsight. There is a list of websites at the end of this chapter.

- Always try to view a property before you pay a deposit or buy. What you see in glossy brochures and on websites may not be the whole picture.

- What is the prospect for future growth? Again, get a clear picture of this very important aspect of investment. Don't rely on the headline figures in advertisements. Many countries are just as prone as we are to boom and bust cycles. Make sure that you have a clear investment plan before committing.

As we have seen, it is now possible to go anywhere almost, and to buy anything, almost. Property investment in a whole range of countries, to suit all pockets, has become the norm. However, it is very important to know yourself well and to know the reasons why you are about to invest in property in another country. If you are not clear why you want to buy, but are attracted to the prospect of owning abroad, then the questions listed below are the ones that you should be asking yourself and reflecting on before making any move at all.

- What are you looking for in a property, do you want a second home, is it for investment and income/capital growth or a combination of these factors?
- Are you looking for an eventual retirement home?
- Is good weather an important factor?
- What do you know about a particular country and its future prospects?
- Will you become bored with a particular project after a time?

If you are planning to move permanently to anther country can you make a living? How well do you know the language and customs of a country?

The point of asking these questions to yourself and to others involved in the project with you is to ensure that you are serious, know the upsides as well as the downsides and know yourself well. If you are choosing to go to another country to live make sure that you will want to be there in several years time. If you are buying a second home for holiday purposes, will you want to keep going back to the same place year in year out? Many who have invested in timeshare for example have found to their detriment that the novelty wears off after a while. The main point to come out of the above is to be very careful, make sure that you know your country well before buying and never give into sales pressure. Sales people are only your friend when you are lining their pockets. After that you are on your own.

The next chapter covers financing a purchase abroad, which underpins the whole process.

****

10

Financing a Purchase Abroad

At the time of writing, the availability of so-called 'cheap' money throughout Europe is scarce. The problems experienced in the United States, have percolated throughout the world and banks are more and more stringent with their lending criteria. Nevertheless, it is still very possible to obtain financing for purchases abroad, albeit on less favourable terms than previously.

Many in the UK traditionally levered equity out of their properties to finance their purchases abroad. Although this is still the case, currently the amount of people doing so has diminished. Many people will still look to the traditional route of raising a mortgage specifically to buy abroad.

The introduction of the euro has altered the situation somewhat. It is now easier to compare prices within these countries when dealing with a single currency. However, at the same time this has resulted in a big demand for properties from Northern Europeans which has tended to drive prices upwards. One factor that needs to be considered is that, no matter what the demand, it is highly unlikely, notwithstanding claims to the contrary from those advertising and selling property, that property prices in Europe generally will see the illogical and ultimately damaging spiraling increases that characterised the UK property market. In fact, given the rapid new build development in European countries, it is likely that prices will go down as well as up, due to over-supply. This trend is now characterising many countries such as Bulgaria (the first of the emerging countries to develop in a big way) and the Baltic States. One other point to consider when purchasing abroad is the actual on-costs of purchasing a property. In most European countries the costs of purchasing are considerably higher than in the UK when factoring in costs such as legal fees, stamp duty (or the equivalent) and other taxes.

Different ways of purchasing property abroad

There are two main ways of purchasing a property abroad, paying cash or raising a mortgage, much as in the UK. The mortgage can be raised either in the UK or abroad. There are a number of special mortgages that can be raised, usually in the country of purchase but also elsewhere raised by brokers. As with the UK, especially now, you will have to prove to a foreign lender that you have sufficient income to repay a mortgage. They will ask for a large amount of proof, more so than UK banks, that this is the case. Whether paying cash or buying on a mortgage you will need a bank account in the country where you purchase which must always be kept in credit.

There are advantages and disadvantages to paying in cash or by mortgage. With cash, of course you will not have to service a long-term loan which will end up costing you much more than the original purchase price of the property. However, when paying in cash, unless you are very careful, you could end up paying a lot for something that is not in fact worth the asking price. When you get a mortgage at least the bank will wish to ensure that the collateral for their loan is secure. Hence they will insist on a thorough survey and will provide advice if the property in their opinion is not worth the price.

Disadvantages of overseas mortgages

It is worth mentioning here that there are several disadvantages to raising mortgages overseas. The main disadvantage is that it is in a foreign currency. This adds a relative layer of risk to your investment. With this set up, you are earning in sterling but paying in a foreign currency therefore you will be liable for any exchange rate fluctuations.. There is also the disadvantage of communication barriers. You will need to visit the country at least once to sort out mortgage matters and you will find barriers which could impact on anything you do or sign.

It is entirely up to you how you raise capital but bear in mind the disadvantages.

Most mortgage lenders will insist that a property has the proper insurance and also many will want you to have life insurance. Remember that they are lending money against a property and against your income and they wish to be safe and see their loan protected. When paying cash it is up to you what you do although most people would take the sensible route and make sure insurance is in place.

When buying a foreign property on a mortgage you will have to have a mortgage inspection report, and pay for this. This is non-refundable and can cost anything up to £500. A qualified surveyor will prepare the report and submit this to the lender. From this report the lender will decide whether or not there is enough security in the property to justify the mortgage being asked for.

Once satisfactory reports have been received you will be offered a loan, in writing, and an offshore company may be set up for the sole purpose of owning the property. This is a convenient way for the banks to lend to a person to buy property in another country.

One typical mortgage arrangement for buying a property abroad is that of Santander UK who will loan up to 75% of the purchase price for property in Spain or Portugal. As in the UK the more you borrow the more you pay. This will exclude legal and other fees which you must find yourself. It is purely against the property. Loans can be arranged for a variety of residential purchases, main residence, second home, buy to let ad so on. However, they will not lend on commercial property. For mortgages on French, Portuguese and Italian properties the process is similar. However, in some countries, such as Italy and Portugal, you will need to hand over around one third of the purchase price. One thing to watch out for is when buying in Spain, the buyer will be saddled with any debts of the seller on completion of purchase.

Lloyds TSB lends money for purchase of property in a range of countries, including France, Spain, Portugal and the US. the minimum you can borrow is £100,000, or the currency equivalent. Barclays lends for properties in France, Spain, Italy, Portugal and South Africa. When looking at property, particularly in Spain or Portugal, where many people have suffered the adverse effects of property laws, you will need to satisfy yourself of the following:

- Are there any major works required on the property and what will the costs be? Are all the services connected? This may sound silly but this is quite often the case when you purchase new build in these countries.

- What will be the impact of future developments on your property. Although the massive development programme, which has led to over development and price falls, in Spain has now slowed it is still important to carry out thorough searches before committing. The property with sea views that you purchased could turn out to be a property with a view of brick walls.
- Is the property within a community development or urbanization scheme which would make community fees payable?

If you are purchasing a property in euros then the monthly payments must also be in euros and these funds must be cleared so that they are available on each repayment date. Whether making payments in euros or sterling your bank account must always be in credit at least two months payments.

Mortgages in Spain and Portugal are typically available for 75% of the purchase price There will be an administration fee to the lender of around £300-£350 refundable only if your application is turned down. Valuation fees, as in the UK, are not refundable. If buying on a mortgage you will be responsible for the lenders legal fees as well as your own. These will typically be around 1% of the purchase price but could vary. Wherever you are buying, you need to provide the following information to mortgage companies:

- Three years tax returns
- P60's for three years
- Payslips for a determined period, usually six months
- If self-employed letters from your accountant
- Three items of credit, such as Visa, Amex etc

- Evidence of mortgage history
- Two reference letters, one from your bank
- Three months bank statements
- Copy of your passport.

Basically, banks abroad are very stringent, much more so than UK banks, although that is changing. You will also need to open a bank account in the country where you wish to buy. Six months mortgage payments must be in this account when the property is purchased.

There are a few other things that it is important to know when purchasing abroad. Check the VAT levels in different countries as sometimes there is a high VAT level levied on new build properties which can raise the purchase price considerably. Check on-costs thoroughly as these are not always advertised by over enthusiastic estate agents. The rule of thumb when buying abroad is that you should add around 10% of the price when working out costs. There are many mortgages around, although as we are seeing these are diminishing, as the true state of the economy is emerging following the onset of the credit crunch. Nevertheless if you are a solid bet you will always get a mortgage.

Using currency brokers

There are many specialist currency brokers around who state that they can achieve a better rate than mainstream banks. Currency brokers buy currency in large amounts so that they can secure better rates than the mainstream banks. Specialist currency brokers will discuss with you the best ways of financing your purchase abroad. If the dealer knows the proposed date of purchase they can then tell you the best rates available at the time. As there are plenty of dealers around you can shop around until you are satisfied that you have the best rate. When you have chosen you then sign a currency contract which will usually entail a fee of around £20-30.

Most ordinary people are now using currency brokers rather than banks to buy properties. If you do intend using such a company then you will need to carry out basic checks of your own before committing:

- Make sure that the company has at least three years audited accounts
- Use a company that specialises in foreign exchange only
- Make sure that the person you are dealing with is a trained broker as the usual high pressure techniques exist in this field as they do elsewhere
- Always get a number of quotes

When buying a property abroad you should bear in mind that even quite small fluctuations in exchange rates can significantly affect the total purchase price of a property.

Taxes

All properties abroad are subject to local taxes, as in the UK. Income declared from rent is taxable. UK residents letting out a property abroad will be liable for UK income tax. Taxes are payable only once so there won't be a double whammy. However, even if tax is not de a return must be made to the authorities in respective countries.

When the property is sold it will be subject to capital gains tax unless it s your own principal home. For details of capital gains tax you should contact HM Revenue and Customs. As a rough guide, if you have owned the home for 10 years 60% of the gain is payable. However, you should contact HMRC for information, as this area is more complex than most people think.

The UK has tax treaties with many countries which allow for exemption from foreign tax as long as this is paid in the UK.

Inheritance tax

If you own a property abroad then inheritance tax matters have to be addressed. Before buying a property abroad you will need sound advice. Generally speaking, it is better to put a property in joint names because in most countries other than the UK inheritance tax is charged on property passed between spouses. In the UK, property can pass between one married partner to another without incurring this tax

If you wish to put your children's name on the property or set up a limited company or trust fund make sure you have good legal advice before you do this. Discover in advance how inheritance tax operates in each country as these differ. For example, in some countries now emerging as desirable locations women are not allowed to own property. This is the case in Islamic countries. If you are interested in buying in an Islamic country find out how these laws will affect you and your inheritance tax position.

You will also need to know whether your foreign property forms part of your UK estate. For example in Spain, Portugal and Italy, as a foreigner you can leave your property according to the rules in your native country. However, in France, Dubai and Turkey even as a foreigner you must abide by the rules of that country. This means for instance that you cannot cut out your children and there is no automatic tax-free inheritance between husband and wife. On buying a foreign property you should make both a new English will and a will that is valid in the country where you have your property.

Different types of market abroad

Markets abroad can be split into three: primary, secondary and tertiary. Primary markets are sophisticated and long established, have a well-developed infrastructure and are places where foreigners have successfully bought property for many years. Secondary markets are less well established, legal structures are not developed and are places where foreigners have only just started to buy. The risks are higher but the returns can be correspondingly higher. Examples of secondary markets are Croatia, Turkey and Dubai.

Tertiary markets are countries or areas where purchase by foreigners has become recently possible, but is not at all established. Properties in tertiary markets will appear to be very cheap but the infrastructure f these countries is very fragile or unknown and the buying process can be very difficult for a number of reasons: the title to land is unclear or may be disputed. Mortgages may not be available and the paperwork may not be valid. These brand new markets represent the highest risk for a potential purchaser. Examples of tertiary markets at the time of writing include Poland, Slovakia, Russia and the Czech Republic. Over time these market will develop but beware when purchasing or looking to purchase a property as there are currently many pitfalls. Get good advice, Go onto the numerous websites which give case histories of people who have bought.

Fractional ownership

Fractional ownership is a relatively new scheme whereby you purchase a fraction of the title deed. Fractional ownership is different to timeshare or holiday clubs where membership is purchased but no title deed. This type of ownership is best suited to holiday homes that are intended to be used for four to six weeks a year. You will get a corresponding share of the title deed entitling you to a certain time. These types of property are typically situated in luxury holiday complexes with sports facilities, such as golf. The management fee payable will also be correspondingly lower as more people are sharing. One point to consider if looking at this type of ownership is that the property is never really yours.

Useful addresses and websites

The Buying Process

The Local Government Association
www.lganet.gov.uk
Confederation of Scottish Local Authorities
www.cosla.gov.uk
Greater London Authority
www.london.gov.uk
The Environment Agency
www.environment-agency.gov.uk
www.homecheckuk.com

House Prices

Halifax www.halifax.co.uk
Nationwide www.nationwide.co.uk
Land Registry www.landreg.gov.uk
www.hometrack.co.uk

Buying agents

Home Search Bureau www.homesearchbureau.com

Property search sites

www.hometrack.co.uk
www.rightmove.co.uk

www.assertahome.co.uk
www.fish4.co.uk
www.propertyfinder.co.uk
www.primelocation.com
www.findaproperty.com
www.08004homes.co.uk
www.thisislondon.co.uk

The buying and selling process

The Law Society www.lawsoc.org.uk
The Council of Mortgage Lenders www.cml.org.uk
HM Customs and Revenue www.inlandrevenue.co.uk

Scotland

Law Society of Scotland www.scotlaw.org.uk

Leasehold/freehold

Lease www.lease-advice.org
Association of Residential Managing Agents
www.arma.org.uk

Mortgage search sites/brokers

Money facts www.moneyfacts.co.uk
www.moneysupermarket.co.uk
www.moneynet.co.uk

New homes

NHBC www.nhbc.co.uk
National Association of New Homeowners www.nanho.org.uk

Auctions
www.propwatch.com

Index

www.straightforwardco.co.uk

All titles, listed below, in the Straightforward Guides Series can be purchased online, using credit card or other forms of payment by going to www.straightfowardco.co.uk A discount of 25% per title is offered with online purchases.

Law
A Straightforward Guide to:
Consumer Rights
Bankruptcy Insolvency and the Law
Employment Law
Private Tenants Rights
Family law
Small Claims in the County Court
Contract law
Intellectual Property and the law
Divorce and the law
Lasting powers of attorney
Leaseholders Rights
The Process of Conveyancing
Knowing Your Rights and Using the Courts
Producing Your own Will
Housing Rights
The Bailiff the law and You
Probate and The Law
Company law
What to Expect When You Go to Court
Guide to Competition Law
Give me Your Money-Guide to Effective Debt Collection

Caring for a Disabled Child

General titles
Letting Property for Profit
Buying, Selling and Renting property
Buying a Home in England and France
Bookkeeping and Accounts for Small Business
Creative Writing
Freelance Writing
Writing Your own Life Story
Writing performance Poetry
Writing Romantic Fiction
Speech Writing
Teaching Your Child to Read and write
Teaching Your Child to Swim
Raising a Child-The Early Years
Creating a Successful Commercial Website
The Straightforward Business Plan
The Straightforward C.V.
Successful Public Speaking
Handling Bereavement
Play the Game-A Compendium of Rules
Individual and Personal Finance
Understanding Mental Illness
The Two-Minute Message
Buying a Used Car
Tiling for Beginners

Go to:
www.straightforwardco.co.uk